What Makes Me A
QUAKER?

Adam Woog

KIDHAVEN PRESS

An imprint of Thomson Gale, a part of The Thomson Corporation

Detroit • New York • San Francisco • San Diego • New Haven, Conn. • Waterville, Maine • London • Munich

THOMSON
™
GALE

*My thanks to Margaret Fraser, Anthony Manousos,
Ben Richmond, Sally Rickerman, Bill Samuel, and Michael
Wadja for their patient answers to my questions.*
AW

For more information, contact
KidHaven Press
27500 Drake Rd.
Farmington Hills, MI 48331-3535
Or you can visit our Internet site at http://www.gale.com

LIBRARY OF CONGRESS CATALOGING-IN-PUBLICATION DATA

Woog, Adam, 1953–
    Quaker? / by Adam Woog.
      p. cm. — (What Makes Me A?)
    Summary: Discusses Quakerism, including how the religion began, what
Quakers believe, and how Quakers practice their faith.
      Includes bibliographical references and index.
      ISBN 0-7377-3082-X (hardcover : alk. paper)
    1. Society of Friends. I. Title. II. Series.
      BX7731.3.W66 2004
      289.6—dc22
                                                                  2004013096

CONTENTS

CHAPTER ONE

How Did Quakerism Begin?

Quakerism is one branch of Christianity. Christianity, one of the world's great religions, is based on the life and teachings of Jesus Christ, who lived about two thousand years ago. Christians believe that Jesus was the Son of God. He taught a message of love, peace, and simplicity.

The Quaker branch is only one small part of the many **denominations** (religious groups) of Christianity. Some Christian denominations have millions of members, but there are currently only about 300,000 Quakers worldwide. Of these, about 130,000 live in the United States.

However, Quakerism's size is misleading. Despite their small numbers, Quakers have had a huge impact on society. This is largely because they believe in acting on their strong religious feelings about such issues as social justice, human rights, and peace.

Quakers have therefore always worked to make the world a better place. For example, early American Quakers played a big role in shaping the U.S. Constitution and the Bill of Rights. Quakers from around the world helped write the United Nations charter. Quakers around the world have made, and still make, important contributions to public education. They also play an important part in the struggle to ensure equal rights for everyone. Throughout their history, the Quakers

Quaker William Penn signs a treaty with a Native American tribe. Quakers have always helped protect the rights of all people.

have lived up to what George Washington said about them: "There is no denomination among us who are more exemplary and useful citizens."[1]

George Fox's Visions

Quakerism began in the 1650s with the teachings of an Englishman, George Fox. Fox was raised in the Puritan faith, a very strict form of Christianity. However, he was unhappy with his faith and was not interested in other denominations he investigated. He felt that their practices and beliefs had become complicated and impersonal, far removed from Jesus's lessons of simplicity and modesty.

Fox passionately wanted a simpler faith, one that could give him a personal and direct connection with God. When he was still a teenager, Fox began wandering around England in search of answers. During this period, he had a series of spiritual visions. He later wrote about one of them, "I heard a voice which said, 'There is One, even Christ Jesus, that can speak to your condition.'"[2]

Fox's visions revealed to him that a part of God's spirit lives in every person. He called this spirit the Inward Light. Fox believed that finding the Inward Light was a way for people to have a direct connection with God.

Fox Gains Followers

Still a young man, Fox wandered the countryside with no permanent home or church, preaching his beliefs. Fox preached wherever he could, talking to people about his concept of the Inward Light.

GEORGE FOX ON THE MOUNT OF VISION—THE VOICE OF ONE CRYING IN THE WILDERNESS

ON THIS MOUNTAIN HE WAS MOVED OF THE LORD TO SOUND OUT HIS GREA

George Fox experiences a spiritual vision on a mountaintop. Fox believed that a part of God's spirit lives in everyone.

Many people were attracted to Fox's message, and they formed groups to study his **sermons** (religious lectures). Within a decade, somewhere between twenty thousand and sixty thousand people became members of the group.

The denomination's official name was (and still is) the Religious Society of Friends. They gave themselves this name because they considered themselves friends of Jesus and "friends of Truth." They were commonly known simply as Friends, a name that is still used today.

There are two stories about the origin of the group's other name. One is that they were called Quakers because

The Cradle of Quakerism

S C O T L A N D

Swarthmoor Hall
Early place of refuge
for the Quaker movement.

North Sea

Lancaster

Firbank Fell
In June 1652, George
Fox preaches to a
gathering of about
one thousand people.
This begins the Quaker
movement.

Irish Sea

Pendle Hill
In May 1652, George Fox
has a vision of a "great
people to be gathered."

U N I T E D

K I N G D O M

London

English Channel

George Fox

they trembled when they prayed. The other story comes from a time when Fox was on trial for **heresy.** (Heresy means speaking against traditional beliefs.) Fox told the judge in the trial that he should quake and tremble at the word of the Lord. Fox wanted the judge to understand his belief that God was the most powerful force in the universe. The judge asked Fox sarcastically if he was a "Quaker." Fox replied that he was, and the name stuck.

More Beliefs

Fox taught many other ideas besides the concept of the Inward Light. One was the importance of being kind to others and of always helping the less fortunate. All Christian churches teach this concept, but the Friends earned a reputation for acting seriously on it.

Fox also believed that people should reject the practices of existing Christian churches, such as their rituals for religious services. He urged his followers instead to worship very simply. Early Quaker services thus had no songs, sermons, or group prayers. They consisted of little besides silent worship.

Fox had advice about other aspects of life as well. He urged his followers to reject pastimes and items that might distract them from a life of worship. Fox advised his followers to give up many activities, including drinking alcohol, playing sports and games, and collecting art. He also was against music, theater, wigs, and jewelry.

Quakers wore simple clothes, symbolizing that one's outward appearance was unimportant. They lived in

Quakers lived in plain houses and wore simple clothes to symbolize that outward appearance is unimportant.

plain houses and worshipped in undecorated buildings. Furthermore, they used distinctive speech, such as "thee" and "thou" instead of "you."

Dangerous Radicals

Many of the Friends' beliefs and practices directly oppose normal customs. For instance, they refuse to swear an oath to tell the truth in court. This is because Quakers feel they should always tell the truth. To them, everyday truth and court truth are the same—and so there is no need to swear an oath.

Quakers also refuse to swear **allegiance** (loyalty) to a king or any other person, insisting that they are loyal only to Jesus. Furthermore, they believe in pacifism. That is, they oppose violence in all forms and refuse to serve in the military.

Because of such beliefs, Quakers were considered dangerous radicals by many church leaders, government authorities, and everyday people. The Friends were severely **persecuted** (treated harshly) as a result. They were sometimes attacked by angry mobs, tortured, or even killed.

More often, they were jailed. Fox was arrested and jailed eight times between 1649 and 1673, spending a total of six years in prison. An estimated fifteen thousand

George Fox visits a family of Friends in prison. Early Quakers were often jailed for their religious beliefs.

other Friends were also jailed between 1660 and 1685 because of their religious beliefs. Almost five hundred of them died in prison (or shortly afterward) as a result of rough treatment there.

Moving On

Persecution caused many Friends to leave England. They sought peace and freedom elsewhere, especially in the American colonies. Life in the colonies was uncertain, rough, and often dangerous. However, to

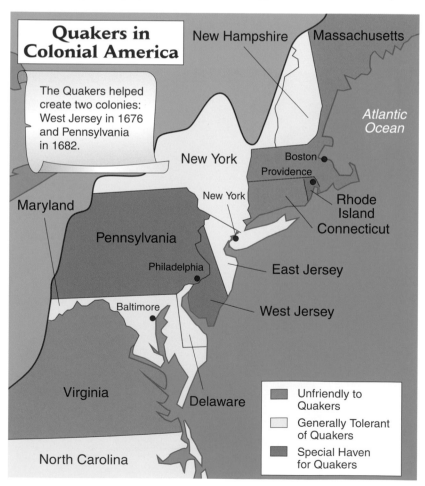

Quakers in Colonial America

The Quakers helped create two colonies: West Jersey in 1676 and Pennsylvania in 1682.

New Hampshire
Massachusetts
Atlantic Ocean
New York
Boston
Providence
New York
Rhode Island
Connecticut
Maryland
Pennsylvania
Philadelphia
East Jersey
Baltimore
West Jersey
Virginia
Delaware
North Carolina

Unfriendly to Quakers
Generally Tolerant of Quakers
Special Haven for Quakers

the Quakers the promise of religious freedom was worth the risk.

Not all of the colonies welcomed them. Places where certain other Christian groups had already settled, such as Massachusetts, were often unfriendly. Some colonists imprisoned, tortured, and even killed Friends who tried to settle near them. One Quaker whose ears had been cut off because of his religious beliefs wrote in 1658, "Great have been the sufferings of Friends in this land."[3]

Some colonies, however, were more tolerant. Among these were Maryland, Delaware, and New York. The Friends found a special haven in Rhode Island. Quakers also helped create two completely new colonies: West Jersey, which later became part of New Jersey, and Pennsylvania, which became so closely linked to the Friends that it is still called the Quaker State.

In those early days, all Quakers held very similar beliefs. However, this has gradually changed over the centuries. Today, Quakerism has expanded to include many variations, but the Friends still share a basic core of spiritual belief set forth by George Fox.

CHAPTER TWO

What Do Quakers Believe?

T he Quaker faith stresses the importance of individual belief and action. As a result, within Quakerism, many separate groups have their own special **doctrines** (formal beliefs). Furthermore, individual Quakers can have very different beliefs from each other, or from the majority of Quakers, and still be considered Quakers. An old joke says that twenty Quakers in a room will have at least twenty different sets of beliefs.

Despite these differences, however, Friends generally share a few fundamental beliefs about ways to worship and live. These beliefs form the heart of Quakerism and are rooted in how the Friends have interpreted Jesus's life and teachings. Quakers often call these shared beliefs testimonies.

The Inward Light

Quakers, for instance, share a basic belief that every person is born with power that is a gift from God and

In this painting, the spirit of Jesus appears during a Quaker meeting.
Quakers believe everyone has a personal connection with God.

is part of him. This power is a source of strength that can be used to make the world a better place. According to Quaker teachings, Jesus possessed unlimited amounts of this sacred power.

George Fox called this inner source of strength the Inward Light. (It is sometimes also called the Inward Seed.) Quakers believe that people can find their own Inward Light if they sit quietly with open hearts, waiting patiently and listening carefully. According to George Fox, "Stand still in the Light, and submit to it, and temptations and troubles will be hushed and gone."[4]

By connecting with the Inward Light, Fox taught, people can experience moments, called openings, when God's spirit speaks to them. When these occur, God directs people to act. Openings can sometimes happen to people when they are alone, but they happen more usually during group worship.

Since every person has access to his or her Inward Light, Quakers believe, everyone can have a personal connection to God. Everyone can therefore directly experience and understand him. Nothing needs to be between God and an individual—not even a **minister** or a church. For Quakers, connecting with God is thus an intensely personal experience.

Equality and Nonviolence

Another basic Quaker belief is the conviction that all people are children of God and equal in his eyes. Because of this, women and men have had equal status in Quaker communities since the denomination's earliest

In this painting, Quakers offer help to escaping slaves. Accepting all people as equal, Quakers were opposed to slavery.

days. Furthermore, Quakers actively oppose racism and other forms of intolerance. Unlike some other religions, Quakerism is tolerant of all people regardless of race, age, nationality, sexuality, or religion.

Belief in the equality of everyone connects directly to one of the best-known aspects of the Quaker faith: a strong belief in pacifism and nonviolence. If everyone is a child of God, and if part of God is within everyone, then violence against another human is violence against God. Quakerism teaches, therefore, that it is wrong to fight.

17

The Quaker view of nonviolence is based on faith in Jesus and in trying to follow his peaceful approach to solving problems. Living a Christian life, George Fox taught, eliminates the need to fight others. When he refused to join the British army, Fox stated, "I told them that I live by that life and power that took away the need for any war."[5]

The Bible

Another belief generally shared by Quakers concerns the importance of the Bible. The Bible, the most sacred book in Christianity, is also sometimes called the Holy Scriptures. It is in two parts—the Old and New Testaments.

The Old Testament, which is ancient, tells stories about God and about the early days of the world. It also predicts the coming of the Son of God. The New Testament, among other things, relates the life and teachings of Jesus. It was written in the years after Jesus's death.

In Christianity, the Bible is the single most important written source of religious knowledge. To some Christians, it is the literal word of God. They believe that everything in the Bible is literally true.

Generally speaking, Quakers agree that the Bible is a sacred and holy text. However, this is open to interpretation. Some Quakers believe that the Bible is the most important spiritual authority. However, many agree with George Fox that God's spirit is more important than the Bible or any human source of knowledge. To them, the Bible is a set of important, inspiring, and powerful lessons and stories. Reading and thinking about these stories can help people listen to what God speaks in their hearts, but the Bible can never be more important than God's spirit itself.

Diverse Opinions

These differences of opinion about the Bible demonstrate an important aspect of the Quaker faith: its diversity. Even the Friends' most basic shared beliefs can be

A group of Quakers marches with banners to protest the war in Iraq. Most Quakers have a strong belief in nonviolence.

open to interpretation. This is because Quakers treasure individuality and personal beliefs so highly.

For example, some Friends are influenced by other sources in addition to the Bible—or even in addition to Christianity. They have brought aspects of Eastern religions and other philosophies into their faith. As a whole, Quakers try to remain open to spiritual insights from many sources, believing that these other sources can also offer rich wisdom.

A Quaker high school student teaches a child to read. The Friends believe it is their duty to help others.

Another example of diversity concerns the Quakers' reputation for pacifism. An opposition to violence is a fundamental part of most Quakers' views. However, some Quaker groups do not stress absolute nonviolence. In the eyes of these groups, for example, it would be possible for a person to defend his or her country by serving in the military and still be considered a Quaker.

Leading a Good Life

All Quakers try to maintain spiritual qualities that will help them lead better, more fulfilling, more useful lives. These qualities include integrity, honesty, simplicity, compassion, and modesty. Quakerism teaches that if people have such qualities, they will have strong individual characters and will be better able to serve others. They will have the inner strength to do good works and lead good lives.

Compassion for others is an especially important personal trait. Quakers believe that actions toward other people should reflect Jesus's love of humanity. However, it is not enough simply to feel compassion toward other people. Quakers also stress the importance of actively helping others through good works.

Quaker beliefs are put into action in several ways. One is to actively aid others. Another is to work for peace. A third is to worship. Like other aspects of their faith, Quakers worship in diverse ways.

CHAPTER THREE

How Do Quakers Practice Their Faith?

Quaker worship services are called meetings for worship, or simply meetings. They are simple services, with few or no elaborate ceremonies. (Even a Quaker wedding is typically very uncomplicated. Often, it is part of a regular worship service, with no rituals beyond the exchange of simple vows between the husband and wife.)

Regular **congregations** (members of specific gatherings) usually fill Quaker meetings. However, the services are always open to non-Quakers. Friends always welcome others who might want to join them.

Where and When

The buildings Quakers use for group worship are called meeting houses. Some denominations call them churches. In keeping with the Quaker belief in simplicity, meeting houses are usually plain, with little or no decoration. For example, there is no cross, which is a familiar symbol in the churches of other Christian religions.

Sometimes a meeting house holds little more than a few rows of benches. These benches are typically arranged in a square or circle. This emphasizes the Quaker belief that everyone is of equal importance. Also, it lets each worshipper be aware of the others.

Worship services usually take place once a week on Sundays. Sunday is the traditional Christian day of rest and worship. Quakers consider it to be the first day of the religious calendar's week.

Quaker meeting houses, like this one in New Jersey, are plain buildings with very little decoration.

A typical meeting begins when the first person enters the room and sits down. Children may be present for a few minutes at the beginning of a meeting. However, they usually have their own activities, such as religious schooling, in another room for most of the time.

Programmed and Unprogrammed

Two basic styles of Quaker worship service have developed over the years: programmed and unprogrammed. In Europe, most services are unprogrammed. In North America, roughly two-thirds of the meetings are programmed, and most of these are newer congregations in the western United States. Elsewhere in the world, programmed meetings are also more common.

Unprogrammed services represent the oldest form of Quakerism. They are not structured, so they have no preset prayers or special Bible readings. Unprogrammed services do not have formal leaders.

Programmed services are more structured. In some ways, they resemble services in other Christian churches. For example, they have a set order of events, including singing, Bible readings, and a sermon. Also, programmed services are typically led by a minister—that is, someone who has received religious training, usually at a special school called a seminary.

Quaker ministers are usually called pastors, or sometimes, recorded pastors. (*Recorded* in this case means recognized by the community.) In addition to leading worship services, pastors typically perform such duties as organizing

This eighteenth-century engraving shows an unprogrammed Quaker service. Such services are unstructured and have no leaders.

group events, supervising property owned by the congregation, or overseeing projects to help the poor.

Silent Prayer

A central part of every worship service, whether it is programmed or unprogrammed, is a period when people sit in silent prayer. They use this time to concentrate on God and to be quiet in their bodies, minds, and spirits.

This silent prayer, which typically lasts about an hour, is called expectant waiting or centering down. By sitting quietly and patiently, people can wait to feel the

A young Quaker prays with her eyes closed during a meeting. Silent prayer is a regular part of Quaker meetings.

presence of God's Spirit. Perhaps their Inward Light will move them in some way. It may reveal a new insight to someone about what is happening in the world. It may reveal sadness to someone about a personal mistake made in the past. Or it may move someone to obey God's Spirit in some other way.

Silent prayer is not always completely silent. Sometimes, people are moved during it to share what is in their hearts. They are free at any time to share these feelings. They can stand up and speak, pray, read aloud, or even sing, provided that what they say has been inspired by God's Spirit.

Ending the Service

After someone speaks, the congregation remains silent for a time. This shows polite respect for what the person has just said, and it gives other people time to think about it. It is rare for someone to speak more than once in a single meeting. No one ever feels pressured to speak out loud. In fact, people are free to remain completely silent if they like.

When an elder (a senior member of the congregation) shakes hands with another person, this marks the

Quakers, like these two women, often gather for coffee and friendly talk after their meetings.

end of the silent period. Other people pick up the handshake, until everyone has shaken hands with those around them. There is no formal time limit on this. People just start shaking hands when it seems right.

A typical Sunday worship service ends with introducing visitors and making announcements, such as notices of forthcoming events or news about absent members. The congregation often then gathers to greet one another informally. Sometimes coffee or lunch is served as well.

For regular members as well as guests, Quaker meetings are peaceful and friendly events. Michael Wajda, associate secretary for development and interpretation for the Friends General Conference, comments, "Many who come into a Quaker meeting for the first time speak of an experience of 'feeling like I've come home.'"[6]

Meetings and Other Gatherings

In addition to their regular worship services, congregations typically have meetings once a month. At these monthly meetings, members of the congregation have a chance to consider a variety of topics. For example, they might discuss applications for new membership. A person who wants to apply typically does so in writing and is invited to meet with a special committee. This committee helps the applicant decide if becoming a Quaker is the right step. If so, approval of an application is usually made at a monthly meeting.

Different congregations within large areas keep in touch by meeting together several times a year, and

A young Quaker speaks out against the death penalty at a conference. Quakers regularly sponsor conferences on important issues.

every year there are big meetings of many congregations. One of the best-known of these is the Philadelphia Yearly Meeting, named for (and held in) a city
that has long been a center for American Quakers.

In addition to worship services and monthly meetings, many congregations sponsor other activities
throughout the year. For example, they might organize
family picnics or hiking trips. They also might sponsor

larger events such as summer camps, workshops on special issues, or spiritual retreats.

Holidays

In the early days, Quakers did not have holidays. They believed that Sunday, the day of group worship, was the only special day that was more sacred than any other. Today, however, many Quakers have less rigid opinions about holidays.

For example, many Friends observe Christmas and Easter, the two most important Christian holidays. Christmas honors Jesus's birth, while Easter honors his death and resurrection. If Quakers do choose to observe

Quaker girls have fun with an art project at summer camp, another type of event Quaker congregations often organize.

these days, they generally do so in the spirit of Quakerism. That is, in keeping with the tradition of simplicity, they concentrate on the main reason for the holidays and avoid any commercialism, such as decorations, gifts, or parties.

Changing Times

The acceptance of holidays is just one example of how Quakerism has changed over the centuries. The split between programmed and unprogrammed meeting styles is another.

Also, the distribution of where Quakers live has changed. Fewer Quakers live in America and England than in past times. Meanwhile, the number of Friends who live in Africa and other developing regions is rising. Such changes will no doubt affect Quakerism as it faces new challenges in the future.

CHAPTER FOUR

What Is the Future of Quakerism?

O ver the centuries, Quakerism has split into several distinct styles. These different branches are shifting in their size and locations. The changes they present will no doubt affect the future of Quakerism.

It is difficult to get exact numbers about membership in the different branches of Quakerism. However, evidence suggests that one main branch is growing quickly. At the same time, membership in another is holding steady or declining slightly.

Growth in Evangelical Quakerism

The branch that is growing quickly is commonly called evangelical Quakerism. Evangelical Quakers attend programmed meetings. As a group, they generally tend to believe more strongly in strict Christian moral values than do unprogrammed Quakers.

Evangelizing means preaching the word of God to others. Evangelical Quakers stress **converting** new members to Quakerism, and they have been very successful at creating new congregations. This is especially true in developing regions such as South America and Africa. Some Quakers in these countries originally came from places like England or America as missionaries, but most members of these congregations are people who already lived there.

A group of young Quakers in Cuba poses for a photo. Evangelical Quakers have won many converts in Latin America and Africa.

The growth of evangelical Quakerism has been especially fast in Africa. Beginning with a few missionaries in Kenya in 1902, the African branch of the Quakers has swelled so much that today more Quakers live in Africa than in North America. They are mostly in Kenya. In fact, Kenya now has more Quakers than any other country in the world, including the United States.

Some observers feel that the growth of Quakerism in regions such as Africa and South America will affect

Quaker pastors teach children in Kenya, Africa, which has more Quakers than any other country in the world.

the future of Quakerism as a whole. For example, Quakers in developing countries will no doubt increasingly bring some of their own distinctive cultures to their religious lives. This multiculturalism may serve to broaden Quakerism's influences.

Holding Steady?

While evangelical Quakerism is growing, there is some evidence that another, older branch of Quakerism may be shrinking. Generally speaking, this branch is made up of Quakers who attend the more traditional form of unprogrammed services. These Quakers are found mainly in Europe and the eastern part of North America.

However, this branch may not actually be shrinking. It appears that many people are coming to meetings even if they are not formal members. Margaret Fraser (the executive secretary of the Friends World Committee for Consultation, Section of the Americas) comments, "I have noticed a pattern in unprogrammed meetings in Europe and North America of a lot of people attending meeting for worship regularly who don't seem to want to join."[7]

A Tradition of Service

No matter what changes take place, Quakers in the days to come will no doubt continue to build on one of their most important traditions. This is their long commitment to serving others. This commitment is built on the Friends' deep religious belief in working for social justice—that is, in putting their faith into action by helping others.

The Friends have always worked hard to make the world a better place. Today, they continue to do so in many ways. Dozens of Quaker-related organizations around the world offer a variety of services.

For example, some groups work to create better conditions in prisons, mental institutions, and workplaces. Others provide services such as agricultural projects in developing countries or medical aid to victims of natural disasters. Still other Quaker-related organizations work to improve human rights, abolish the death penalty, and influence decisions at the United Nations. And there are groups that perform such valuable services as helping homeless kids, providing services for the aging, and promoting environmental awareness.

The AFSC

Connected to the Quaker tradition of service is their work in promoting world peace. To Quakers, it is not enough simply to preach nonviolence or to avoid it. It is equally important to work hard to create a peaceful world.

Of the several Friends-related organizations devoted to peace activism, the best known is the American Friends Service Committee (AFSC). The AFSC began in World War I. During that conflict, many American Quakers wanted to serve their country, but they could not fight in the military. The AFSC provided alternatives for these Quakers. For example, it organized ambulance corps and medical help for civilian war victims.

Teenage Quakers help rebuild an Alabama church. Community service is very important to Quakers.

The organization continued its work during World War II. In 1947, after that conflict ended, the AFSC and its British counterpart were given a great honor. They were awarded the Nobel Peace Prize for their efforts. The two organizations accepted the award on behalf of all Quakers.

American Friends Service Committee members rebuild a house in France destroyed during World War I.

Today, the AFSC is a large organization with staff members who come from many faiths. It oversees dozens of smaller organizations and specific projects. Not all of them are directly connected to peace. Among its other organizations are projects to oppose the death penalty, reform immigrant labor practices, and help the homeless.

The AFSC is the source of some controversy within Quakerism. Not all Quakers support the organization. Some Friends object to what they feel is the AFSC's support of radical and violent liberation movements in some parts of the world, such as the Middle East and Africa.

A Heritage of Education

Education is another important way in which Friends can serve themselves and others. They do this by teaching Quaker standards to children and young adults. To foster this, Friends have founded dozens of schools and universities around the world.

For example, they maintain Friends schools around the world. These typically are for children from kindergarten through twelfth grade. They stress such topics as peace, solving conflicts, religious matters, and service to others.

A Palestinian girl works on a problem in a Quaker school in the West Bank. Quakers have established schools throughout the world.

Quakers have also founded a number of major colleges and universities. Among them are such important institutions as Cornell, Swarthmore, Johns Hopkins, and Bryn Mawr. In addition, individual Quaker meetings sponsor many spiritual retreats and workshops on a variety of topics throughout the year.

Education, peace projects, and other service work represent just a few aspects of the Quaker tradition of helping others. This tradition of service will no doubt continue well into the future. Quakerism may change to reflect changes in the world and in its own makeup. No matter how it evolves, however, Quakerism in the future will still be a vital religion and an important voice for social change.

NOTES

Chapter One: How Did Quakerism Begin?

1. Quoted in Margaret H. Bacon, *The Quiet Rebels: The Story of the Quakers in America*. New York: BasicBooks, 1969, p. 75.

2. Quoted in Jean Kinney Williams, *The Quakers*. New York: Franklin Watts, 1998, p. 19.

3. Quoted in Daisy Newman, *Procession of Friends: Quakers in America*. Garden City, NY: Doubleday, 1972, p. 32.

Chapter Two: What Do Quakers Believe?

4. Quoted in Hugh Barbour and J. William Frost, *The Quakers*. New York: Greenwood, 1988, p. 39.

5. Quoted in Quakerism, "Quakerism: A Religion Meaningful for Today's World," www.quakerinfo.org/quakeris.htm.

Chapter Three: How Do Quakers Practice Their Faith?

6. Michael Wajda, e-mail message to author, May 20, 2004.

Chapter Four: What Is the Future of Quakerism?

7. Margaret Fraser, e-mail message to author, May 17, 2004.

GLOSSARY

allegiance: Loyalty.

congregation: The people who attend an individual church.

converting: Bringing new members to a religious group.

denomination: A specific religious group or religion.

doctrines: Accepted beliefs or teachings.

evangelizing: Spreading religious education by telling other people.

heresy: Saying something that goes against standard teachings or beliefs.

ministers: Protestant religious leaders. Some denominations call their leaders pastors.

persecuted: To be treated badly because of religious beliefs.

sermon: A lecture during a church service on some religious subject.

FOR FURTHER EXPLORATION

Books

Marlene Tark Brill, *Allen Jay and the Underground Railroad.* Minneapolis: Carolrhoda, 1993. A story about a real-life Quaker boy whose family became part of the secret Underground Railway, helping slaves escape in the 1840s.

Steven Kroll, *William Penn: Founder of Pennsylvania.* New York: Holiday House, 2000. A biography of America's most famous Quaker.

Eileen Lucas, *Prudence Crandall: Teacher for Equal Rights.* Minneapolis: Carolrhoda, 2001. A nicely illustrated book for young readers about an American Quaker of the 1800s who fought to give everyone, including slaves, a good education.

INDEX

PICTURE CREDITS

ABOUT THE AUTHOR

Adam Woog is the author of over forty books for adults, young adults, and children. He grew up in Seattle, Washington, and lives there now with his wife and their daughter.